Cleverest Comebacks

**Philip Yates &
Matt Rissinger**
Illustrated by Rob Collinet

Sterling Publishing Co., Inc.
New York

To Joe Medeiros, our mentor and Comic Muse. Thanks for
teaching us how to be funny.

—M.R. & P.Y.

Library of Congress Cataloging-in-Publication Data
Yates, Philip, 1956-
  Cleverest comebacks ever! / Philip Yates & Matt Rissinger ;
illustrated by Rob Collinet.
    p. cm.
  ISBN 1-4027-1076-3
  1. Wit and humor, Juvenile. 2. Invective–Juvenile humor. I.
Rissinger, Matt. II. Collinet, Rob. III. Title.

PN6166.Y38 2005
818'.5402–dc22

2005010574

10 9 8 7 6 5 4 3 2 1

Published by Sterling Publishing Co., Inc.
387 Park Avenue South, New York, NY 10016
© 2005 by Matt Rissinger and Philip Yates
Distributed in Canada by Sterling Publishing
$^c/_o$ Canadian Manda Group, 165 Dufferin Street
Toronto, Ontario, Canada M6K 3H6
Distributed in Great Britain and Europe by
Chris Lloyd at Orca Book Services,
Stanley House, Fleets Lane, Poole BH15 3AJ, England
Distributed in Australia by Capricorn Link (Australia) Pty. Ltd.
P.O. Box 704, Windsor, NSW 2756, Australia

Printed in China
All rights reserved

Sterling ISBN 1-4027-1076-3

For information about custom editions, special sales, premium and
corporate purchases, please contact Sterling Special Sales
Department at 800-805-5489 or specialsales@sterlingpub.com.

Contents

Introduction—
Know Excuses!

What do an upset stomach and a class clown have in common? That's easy. They both answer you back.

A good answer is better than a blank stare. A good answer shows you have wit, intelligence, and all the makings of the next great comedian. It also shows that you don't take life so seriously and that a funny comeback will win you a laugh instead of a day in detention.

Well, maybe a laugh *and* a week in detention. But what's wrong with a week in detention as long as you have a book like this to keep you company? Just think of the hours you'll spend memorizing each and every one of these clever retorts.

In fact, maybe there's even an excuse for getting you out of detention, too. (See page 35 for ideas)

Packed inside this book is an arsenal of answers with attitude. So, when it comes to comebacks, remember—leave no answers unturned.

1. Class Classics

Can you calm down?

Yes. Will I? No.

Why? Hyperventilating gives skin a healthy glow.

Please, you first.

Why? Is there a rule here against climbing the walls?

My brain is calm but it takes my body a while to catch up.

Strange—your mouth is moving but I can't tell if it's you that's talking.

This *is* calm. You should see me *before* my yoga class.

Are you two having a staring contest?

No, we're just trying to see eye to eye.

Yes, but if you blink you'll miss it.

No, we are extremely nearsighted.

No, we are two androids trying to get a
telepathic tune-up.

No, we're hypnotizing each other, and I'm not
sure who's winning.

Yes, and the winner gets to swap eyeballs.

You know what they say—stare and stare alike.

No, it's a new Boy Scout trick. By rubbing noses
together we can start a fire.

No, we're doing quality control inspections on
each other's contact lenses.

Are you washing your hands?

No, I'm giving the sink a drink.

No, I'm testing to see if this soap really floats.

No, I'm making a water slide for my fingers.

Yes, if I can find them beneath all this dirt.

Yes, it's a once-a-year tradition.

No, I just find the sound of running water relaxing.

Yes, I'm washing my hands of everything!

I just had my palm red and I'm trying to get it back to its original color.

What did you bring for show-and-tell?

Say hello to my cousin, the Invisible Man.

Me! After all, I've been absent for a week so I thought you might want to take a good look at what you missed.

I brought an atom, the building block of the universe. You can see it, can't you?

Go ahead—pass them around. They're the prize-winning entry in the World's Stinkiest Sneakers competition.

That time machine really works! Show-and-tell was two weeks ago.

Why are you talking in the library?

Shh, the principal sent me here to find out if you're doing your job.

It's not me. Some other kid is throwing his voice in my direction.

Well, séances require talking in order to communicate with the world beyond.

Sorry, this book I'm reading is all about how to give a speech.

That's my imaginary friend talking. He warned me you'd be coming over.

I'm not talking; it's the metal filling in my tooth picking up radio stations all over the world. Wanna hear Brazilian rock?

Maybe you're hallucinating. Have you seen any little green men or pink elephants yet?

Where are you going? This is a test.

The instructions said this is timed, so I'm going to the gym to get a stopwatch.

Oh, I thought it was a pop-up quiz.

Yes, it's a test on the American Revolution, so I decided to rebel and not take it.

I left the answers I copied from your desk inside my locker.

I need a breath of fresh failure.

The principal asked me to dust the fire alarm for fingerprints.

I'm really into passing, so I'm passing this one up.

I have to step into the hallway and consult with the ghost of Albert Einstein.

I forgot my cell phone. I need to call 1-800-Help-Me-Pass.

I'm going swimming. After all, you said this is an open-brook test.

Oh, I thought you said, "nest." I was heading out to hatch some eggs.

How can I cheat when I forgot my binoculars?

Are you having a cookout?

No, I'm just giving these hot dogs a suntan.

Yes, there was too much smoke in the kitchen, so I decided to cook outside.

Must you always grill me with these questions?

No, I'm sending smoke signals for help.

No, I'm conducting a science experiment on global warming.

Yes, are you hungry? The s'more the merrier.

Why didn't you show your work?

I used invisible ink on my imaginary calculator.

I'm trying to conserve energy—mine.

They don't call me the International Man of Mystery for nothing!

I was doing my homework in the kitchen when my mother accidentally used it to make math potatoes.

With my superior brain this wasn't work—merely child's play.

Because my father said I had nothing to show for myself.

Hey, I thought we were having math class, not show-and-tell.

Did you really write this excellent paper?

I can't take all the credit, but I will.

Yes, I wrote down everything my dad said.

No, but I did write a check to pay for it.

Yeah, ain't me a excerlant stodint?

Well, part of the credit should go to the website.

Yes, it was in the best book I ever copied from.

Someone else's name is on it, but I'll accept the A in his absence.

I had a little help from a Ouija board.

Why are you always daydreaming in science class?

I'm trying to come up with a formula to make homework disappear.

I'm not daydreaming. I'm holding a séance with dissected frogs.

Interesting finding—whenever I don't pay attention, you have the same reaction.

Sorry, my father is a snowplow driver and I tend to drift off.

Science class! No wonder I can't find my place in this math book.

If you hadn't interrupted, I would have figured out a solution to world hunger.

Why are you always talking when I'm talking?

Because I'm Jabber the Hut.

Because someone here has to make sense.

Oh, sorry. I thought this was public speaking class.

What did you say? I didn't hear you; I was talking.

Because the principal said I had to repeat this class over and over again.

I'm practicing for a crowd scene in the school play.

Are you talking to me?

Why do you have your head on the desk?

I misplaced my neck.

It's really my book bag camouflaged to look like a human head.

Because my feet wouldn't fit.

You told us to get down to work.

I forgot my contacts, and the graffiti on this desk is so small.

Didn't you just say we should start using our heads?

Why didn't you do your homework?

I got temporary amnesia and I forgot. What was your question?

My cat did it for me, but it's in her language.

My clone did it, but he's out sick today.

My dog ate it, and then my science fair project ate my dog.

I did, but it fell into a spy's hands.

My parents were abducted by aliens and they took my homework with them.

I did a report on worms and my uncle used it as bait.

Why are you closing your eyes during the test?

Didn't you say not to let other pupils look at our papers?

I need a miracle and I'm praying to pass.

Just taking a shot in the dark.

I was hoping I would fall back to sleep and realize this was just a bad dream.

I'm conjuring up the spirit of Nostradamus. He always predicts the right answers.

"Test?" I thought you said, "Rest."

How did you get out of detention?

I pleaded temporary insanity.

My father taught me to always carry a parachute.

I told them you did it.

I bet the teacher you would ask me a stupid question.

I threatened to reveal the main ingredient in the cafeteria meat loaf.

It helps to have a twin brother.

Why is your homework folder empty?

My homework on the solar system fell into a black hole.

Oh, no, termites must be snacking in my backpack.

You said, "Write about what you know."

It's a book report on the Invisible Man.

It's a report about the energy crisis—mine.

It's a paper about ESP; you'll have to read my mind.

Why didn't you make the honor roll?

I did, but they wrote my name in invisible ink.

I prefer a hot dog roll instead.

It's the principal's fault. He keeps me so long in his office.

I did, and it rolled right out the door.

I thought A's and B's were blood types.

I did make the honor roll. When I pleaded not guilty, you should have seen the judge's eyes roll.

How was detention?

About three hours.

It was pretty good until the principal caught us trying to tunnel out.

It was so much fun I might go back again tomorrow.

Great! We got extra credit for sleeping quietly.

One more hour and I might have invented a cure for dry skin.

Thank goodness they left the window open, or we couldn't have gone out for ice cream.

I couldn't believe what great reception I got on my miniature TV.

2. No Sweat

Are you exercising?

No, I'm running away from my obligations.

Yes, I want to get thin so I can get a job as a scarecrow.

Yes, my doctor put me on a seven-day diet, and I ate the whole thing in one day.

No, I'm pedaling this stationary bike because I'm too lazy to go anywhere.

Do you call that dancing?

Why, hasn't it started raining yet?

No, I call it a picnic with ants.

No, I call it, "He must be crazy—we better send him home from school right away!"

No, I call it 9.1 on the Richter scale.

What's wrong with having a little spring in your feet?

No, I call it, "Possessed by the Ghost of Elvis Presley."

No, this is my impression of the world's first human jackhammer.

No, I've just gone swimming and I'm trying to get the water out of my ear.

No, I'm the first human blender. Care for a shake?

No, didn't you hear, today's National Stomp Out Cockroaches Day?

No, it's so hot in here I'm trying to stir up a breeze.

No, the planet where I come from we call it, "Nanu-Nanu!"

No, I'm practicing for that day when somebody tells me to "Go jump off a cliff!"

No, I call it the after-effects of a pogo stick.

Are you all playing Hacky Sack?

No, we just walked across a nest of killer bees.

No, we skipped school today. We're really playing hooky sack.

No, we're experimenting with new ways to toss pizza dough.

No, it's an alien life form. If it touches Earth we'll all die.

Yes, we're playing Hacky Sack—except the guy in the middle. He stopped to ask for directions.

Actually, we couldn't find a Hacky Sack, so we're using the cafeteria meat loaf.

Are you tap dancing?

No, my nutcracker broke.

No, I just painted my toenails and I'm trying to dry them off.

No, I'm skipping with an invisible rope.

No, I'm using Morse code to order a pizza.

No, I'm trying to attract woodpeckers.

Tap dancing? I'm trying to kill all these cockroaches.

Dancing? No, I 'm scraping gum from the bottom of my shoe.

Are you building a tree house?

No, it's a habitat for giant squirrels.

No, this tree is sick and my acupuncturist recommended I stick a few nails in it.

Yes, and won't Mom and Dad be surprised when they find out I borrowed their sofa?

Yes, but don't tell the neighbors I'm using their tree.

No, it's a shelter for underprivileged owls.

No, it's a high-rise hideout from bullies.

Well, I wouldn't go out on a limb and call it a tree house.

No, I'm building a trap for these bears who've been raiding our refrigerator.

Why are you carrying a shovel?

This isn't a shovel, it's a spoon. I promised my friend Emily Elizabeth to feed her big, red dog.

I'm about to start out for China.

Shh! You haven't seen a treasure map blow by here, have you?

Today is Hippie Day at school. You dig, man?

My dad lost his car keys and said, "Leave no stone unturned."

My pet rock passed away, and I'm off to bury him.

Even though it's August, I want to be the first on my block to make money shoveling snow.

Are you going skiing?

No, I'm returning these shoes to the store. They're ten feet too long for my feet.

Yes, it's really hot out and I thought I'd slide down the sun's rays.

Yes, I hear it's the most convincing way to break your leg and get out of school.

Yes, my teacher says if my grades don't get better I'm going downhill fast.

No, it's a new way of surfing.

No, these are giant tongue depressors for oversized humans.

No, I'm on the football team and these are my punting shoes.

Yes, skiing always gives me a lift.

3. Dips and Drips

Why did you get sent to the principal's office?

I won first prize for most detentions in one year.

My teacher thought it would be a good idea for someone to keep him company.

I told the teacher I had a strong interest in travel.

He asked me to help redecorate his office.

I thought I'd save him time, so I sent myself.

The principal wants to adopt me.

Didn't you hear? I'm his new bodyguard.

Hurry up! Are you trying to drink the water fountain dry?

I'm not drinking. I'm practicing holding my breath underwater.

I need a lot of water. You did say I was a big drip, didn't you?

Yes, I'm trying to drink it dry. I'm really a camel in disguise.

Patience, please. I'm teaching my pet worm to water ski.

Water fountain! I thought this was a pencil sharpener. No wonder the point is so soggy.

No, I'm throwing a splash party for my tongue.

No time for idle chitchat! The school's on fire and the sprinkler system is clogged.

No, but if I leave it on long enough, it'll fill the swimming pool.

Yes, my science teacher says our bodies are 80 percent water, and I want to get it up to 100.

No, I decided that if the cafeteria food won't send me home sick, the rusty water will.

No, I'm practicing for my first scuba diving adventure.

No, my nose is stuck to a piece of bubble gum.

No, this is how I always clean my contact lenses.

Is that your beautiful new baby brother?

No, the amusement park loaned me this
holographic doll.

Yes, but not nearly as beautiful as this drool on
my coat.

Yes, I'm taking him to the zoo to see if they're
interested.

Why don't you ask him? When he spits up once
it means no. Twice means yes.

No, it's my father. He's taking reducing pills.

Is that the doorbell ringing?

No, I think the cat swallowed the cell phone.

No, I'm watching the *Wizard of Oz,* and they just came to that part about "Ding Dong the Wicked Witch . . . ."

Yes, but don't firemen usually just break down the door?

Yes, but isn't it Dad's turn not to answer it?

Yes, I think the dog invited his friends for a scratch over.

Yes, but I thought you gave the pizza delivery guy his own key.

No, that's the bell for the microwave. I think my sneakers are dry.

Are you sure you're all right? It stopped ringing over an hour ago.

Are you making a Valentine's Day card?

No I'm cutting out hearts 'cause some day I want to be Dr. Frankenstein.

Yes, take a look at it now because you'll never see it again.

No, this is a Just Get Lost card. You don't have to wait till I'm finished.

No, I'm making flash cards for the broken-hearted.

No, I lost all my crayons except red and white.

No, I don't celebrate Valentine's Day. I think it's a really cupid holiday.

No, it's a card for St. Patrick's Day. I just don't like green.

No, I'm studying to be a heart surgeon.

Yes, it's for my teacher. I'm hoping she'll have the heart to pass me.

Are you the safety patrol?

No, these hand signals are a new form of aerobics.

No, I'm the hazard patrol. Get ready to run when the Don't Walk light flashes.

No, neon orange is my favorite color, so I wear it every day.

No, I collect badges as a hobby.

No, I'm an alien from Planet Popcorn; take me to your kernel.

Yes. Are you looking for a trip to the principal's office?

No, I'm the superintendent and I'm undercover.

No, I'm the safety Pa-Troll. You can't cross this bridge, Billy Goat Gruff.

Are you washing the car?

Yes, I'm hoping the cops won't recognize it.

No, I'm just scraping the bugs off the bumper so I can give them a proper burial.

No, I'm massaging it. It has a lumpy bumper.

No, I'm trying to give it a drink, but it doesn't seem to be thirsty.

No, I'm just exercising my pet sea sponge.

Yes, a car always runs better when it looks good.

No, stand back. The car has rabies and it's foaming at the mouth.

No, I'm washing a hippopotamus with wheels.

No, I'm filling it up with water to make the world's weirdest aquarium on wheels.

Are you building a snowman?

No, this is our entry in the World's Biggest Drip competition.

No, we're just into stacking snow.

No, our refrigerator's broken and we're just trying to chill this carrot.

No, this is the world's largest snow cone.

Yes, we tried building a chicken but we couldn't get it to cross the road.

Shh! He thinks he's a real person.

Yes, now can you just chill out with all the questions?

No, it's a scarecrow, for keeping away pesky penguins.

No, I'm making slow-melting bowling balls.

Yes, and I'm taking him to a party because I hear he's a real ice-breaker.

No, I'm making a bodyguard to protect me from the school bully.

Yes, but she's actually a woman. That's why I call her Snow White.

No, I'm painting these boulders white and creating the world's most sought after sculpture.

Yes, but don't worry, it'll blow over.

Is it raining outside?

Does it ever rain inside?

No, the drama club is testing out its new special effects machine.

No, a hundred kids just shook up soda cans and dropped them all at once.

I don't know—I'll man the lifeboats while you get the life jackets ready.

No, I think the school just hit an iceberg.

Can you spell "monsoon"?

No, the new janitor installed the fire sprinklers on the outside of the building.

Did you do something bad to be in detention?

I'm not in detention. The principal asked me to keep an eye on things after school.

No, I made honor roll, and this is the reward.

I wasn't bad, but the python I put in the principal's car was.

Bad? No. Horrible, horrendous, horrific, yes.

Yes, and if you watch and say what I do, you too can be in detention.

No, this is the only place where I can get any privacy.

No, the chairs are more comfortable there than in my homeroom.

No, the library's so noisy, this is the only place to find peace and quiet.

My teacher's so strict, she sends you here if you don't have a No. 2 pencil.

No, I did something good: I stole from the rich kids and gave to the poor ones.

Is this the zoo?

No, it's a prison for creature criminals.

Yes, can't you read the sign? It says, "Don't Feed the Principal."

No, it's a costume party and everyone's dressed up as animals.

No, we're at school, can't you tell? The gorilla is the principal, that giraffe is our gym teacher....

No, it's my science fair project on endangered species. Do you think I'll win first place?

Yes, and with your laugh, they might put you in the hyena cage.

Are you watering the garden?

Yes, you did ask me to wash the lettuce, didn't you?

No, I'm building Wave World for boll weevils.

No, I'm teaching ladybugs to swim.

No, I'm giving the scarecrow a shower.

No, I'm creating a bathhouse for beavers.

No, I'm whipping up a mud facial for you.

No, I'm showing these worms what happened to the *Titanic.*

Yes, and I can't seem to get these plastic roses to grow.

Yes, it's about time the snails got a house-cleaning.

No, I'm re-creating Noah and the Flood, but in miniature.

No, I'm putting out the fire ants.

Yes, I'm getting ready for the Summer Weeding Program.

No, it's a splash party for bullfrogs.

4. Question-able Behavior

How can you do so many stupid things in one day?

Just a spoonful of "stupid" medicine and I'm set for the day.

I get up early.

You have to be organized if you want to get ahead.

Isn't today April Fools' Day?

I'd give you an exact figure if I knew how to work a calculator.

Are you checking for mail in the mailbox?

No, the mailman lost his wristwatch and I was helping him find it.

No, I'm following a big white rabbit who keeps shouting, "I'm late, I'm late!"

No, I'm checking for my latest secret agent assignment from the President.

No, I'm dusting for fingerprints to see if our nosy next door neighbor has been snooping again.

No, I'm checking for a pizza. The delivery man is very nearsighted.

No, I'm installing a video camera so I can see when I get mail.

No, there's a deranged elf on the loose and he might be hiding in here.

No, on my home planet this is where we store the mustard.

No, there's a mouse that lives in this box that gives good manicures.

Yes, our mail isn't very interesting, so I check other people's mail.

This isn't a mailbox. It's a solar-powered bread-baking machine.

No, this is where I camp out at night.

How come you're not laughing at my jokes?

Because I haven't heard one yet.

Let me take off my headphones and you can try again.

I'm sorry, my funny bone is malfunctioning.

My dog told me the same one this morning.

The Driver Ed teacher told me to avoid cracking up.

The last time I laughed at one of your jokes I spent a week in detention.

I laughed so fast you didn't see it. Let's check the instant replay.

Are you scared?

Yes, I'm a regular Rock of Jell-O.

Yes, I'm so nervous, I keep coffee awake.

Yes, I have the guts of a skeleton.

Yes, and they call me Jigsaw. Every time I get scared, I go to pieces.

Yes, I'm a self-made mouse.

No, I shake like this all the time.

No, my knees knock whenever I'm really calm.

Why do you talk so much?

I'm practicing so I can rent my mouth out as a fly catcher.

My vocabulary is small, but my turnover is terrific.

I'm a person of few words—a few million, in fact.

I can't help it. I throw my tongue into high gear before my brain turns over.

When all is said and done—I keep on talking.

Because I can hardly wait to hear what I'm going to say next.

That's not me. It's my other two personalities.

Why don't your exam answers make sense?

What a coincidence. I was going to ask you the
same thing about the exam questions.

They seemed OK when I copied them from the
person next to me.

I have a new system: heads—false, tails—true.

You said we had to fill in the bubbles, and that's
what I did.

Wasn't it a test on the state of chaos in our
world? Then they make perfect sense.

You have to hold them up to a mirror.

They make perfect sense if you understand the
new language I invented.

They do. I sold all my exam answers and made
seventy-five cents.

Are you easy to get along with?

Yes, I'm very easy to get along with—once you learn to follow me.

Yes, of course. Now, can you buy me lunch?

I don't know. By the way, will you take my place in detention tomorrow?

Yes, but only every other day.

Keep being my human shield, and I'll always be easy to get along with.

Yes, just ask the school bully.

Why are you so disagreeable?

Because the doctor says I'm very sneer sighted.

I think I must have gotten up on the wrong side of the Earth this morning.

Because I like sticking my no's in other people's business.

Are you kidding? I'm as tranquil as a Texas cyclone.

I'm practicing to be an umpire.

Because I think the world is against me—and it is.

I'm just doing my impression of the school cafeteria food.

Why must you always be the center of attention?

Who wants attention? Hey, you, I'm over here!

Better attention than detention.

After all, that's a supermodel's job, isn't it?

When I was born, the doctor threw a bright light on me. I've been hooked ever since.

I tried being the center of the universe but the extra gravity made me giddy.

Because I'm not very at good playing shortstop.

Why must you always ask me stupid questions?

I'm not always the center of attention.
Sometimes I like to get some sleep.

Are you really that lazy?

Ask me again when I wake up.

Let me put it this way—instead of walking in my sleep, I hitchhike.

Yes, that's why I need two school desks—one for each foot.

Yes, I'm hoping to beat Rip Van Winkle's record.

Of course not. In fact, I just bought *How to Conquer Laziness* and wondered if you would read it to me.

Yes, I even get winded playing chess.

Yes, that's why I gave up caffeine. It keeps me up the rest of the day.

Are you kidding? Loafing is hard work.

Are you playing with fireworks?

No, the room always lights up when I enter it.

No, my mom says I have a short fuse.

No, this is our July Fourth rain dance ceremony.

Yes, and I'm getting a real bang out of it.

Yes, it does wonders for my sparkling personality.

I'm sorry, I can't hear you. I'm playing with fireworks.

No, I'm trying to scare the cat out of the tree.

No, I'm practicing for my trip to the moon.

Why did you open the window?

So Superman can get a running start.

You don't want my boomerang to break the glass, do you?

How else can I catch snowflakes on my tongue?

It wasn't me; my imaginary playmate needed some air.

I'm expecting a message, and the pigeon is due back any minute.

Because the school bus driver said if I'm late coming out the door again, he won't wait.

To vent the vapor cloud from my chemistry experiment. You don't feel light-headed, do you?

Why are you always sharpening your pencil?

It's not my pencil I'm sharpening, it's my nails.

I like to get right to the point.

So I won't have to listen to any stupid questions.

This is my detention—to sharpen 30 pencils in 60 minutes or was it 60 pencils in 30 minutes?

This is my way of saying, "School is getting to be a real grind."

Because I don't have any teeth left from gnawing the previous pencils.

5. Grown-up Grumpies

Why don't you sit in your seat?

I'm practicing to be an exchange student, and right now I'm exchanging seats.

I will—once we get to school.

I can't scream as loud sitting down.

Because my dad wants me to be a stand-up kind of student.

Sorry, I just can't lower myself to do that.

Did you make those marks on the floor?

No, I think they were made by a dinosaur nearly fifty million years ago.

Yes, now we can find our way around the house by following the footprints.

Yes, would you like me to teach you how to do it?

It's my imaginary playmate again!

Yes, but I'm sure the dog will lick them off.

No, that's the new tile I installed for your birthday!

No, they can't be mine. I always sign my name next to mine.

If I tell the truth will you promise to ground me when school starts?

My marks are low but they're not quite on the floor yet.

You're not going to wear that outfit, are you?

Only if you don't like it.

How else will the international spy I'm supposed to meet recognize me?

Yes, but only every other day. The other days I'll wear the other outfit you don't like.

No, but only if we can go to the mall and buy outrageous designer earmuffs.

Is your dad changing a tire?

Yes, this one isn't flat enough.

It seems to me you don't know jack.

Yes, he's putting on the new "chameleon" tire; it's guaranteed to change itself.

Yes he's a lovable old lug.

No, he needs that rusty nail for his collection.

Yes, it's a hobby of his. He's trying to qualify for a NASCAR pit crew.

That's my mom. Dad's inside changing the baby.

No, he's practicing for the World Strongman competition.

Is that make up I see on your face?

Oh, no I'm melting!

This isn't my face. I borrowed it from a magazine.

No, it's dust. I forgot to vacuum my forehead this morning.

Yes, I missed a history test and the teacher told me today was a make up.

No, it's crop dusting powder. I'm going out now to buzz a corn field.

No, I think it's chalk dust on your glasses.

Yes, and I want to thank you for lending me your compact.

Do you call this cleaning your room?

Let me shove the rest of my clothes under the bed and then I'll answer your question.

No, I call this distracting your attention from my recent report card.

No, I call it a work of art.

I don't know—ask the rats.

Shhh! Don't wake the trash—it's sleeping.

No, somebody else cleaned it. I'm putting it back to normal.

Why are you still sitting in that chair?

That's not a chair. I'm an alien with six legs.

Someone tied my sneakers to the chair legs.

I'm just playing freeze tag.

Why are you still standing there?

I'm demonstrating Einstein's Theory of Revolving Laziness.

I'm actually a hologram. You'll find the real me upstairs going through your wallet.

I'm practicing for my dentist appointment.

I'm hoping to make a good impression.

I'm getting ready for a week of detention.

Can I help it if someone left an open tube of glue on it?

Because I don't have a leg to stand on.

This isn't a chair. It's a booster rocket, and I'll see you on the moon.

Did you catch that fish?

No, I talked him into giving himself up.

No, I was sitting here minding my own business when the crazy thing jumped into my pail.

No, it's a plastic model to get people like you to start conversations.

No, the fish caught *me*.

Yes, I caught him off guard.

No, he waved a white flag and surrendered.

His family turned him in.

Yes, we had a race, and I caught him.

Yes, I was teaching my worm to swim, and this one opened his mouth.

Are you here to see the doctor?

No, I'm here to catch up on my old-magazine reading.

No, I'm here to wipe my muddy shoes all over this nice carpet.

No, I'm here to see you. I heard you call the shots around here.

No, I was just in the neighborhood and thought I'd stop by for a bandage.

Yes, and I brought my sleeping bag, in case he doesn't get around to me until tomorrow.

No, I'm here to visit some perfect strangers.

Yes, I'm not happy with my last disease, and I'd like to trade it for a new one.

6. Say Watt?

Why do you look so familiar?

You may have seen my picture on the post office Most Wanted board.

You might have fed me peanuts at the local zoo.

I don't know—do you collect bugs as a hobby?

I won first place in the Detention Race.

I can't tell without my glasses on.

Are you having your palm read?

She tried reading my mind, but it was blank.

Yes she's giving me answers about the future. You know finals are tomorrow.

No, I'm having it washed; it's sticky from the cotton candy.

No, I'm having a splinter removed.

No, I borrowed somebody else's palm.

No, I'm having a manicure by the light of a crystal ball.

What were you thinking?

Who are you accusing of thinking?

I don't know—my train of thought doesn't have a caboose.

I'm not thinking—I'm possessed by the Ghost of Christmas Past.

How much it would cost to have your clever brain exchanged for mine.

I was wondering how much money was in your wallet.

Who's thinking? I'm walking in my sleep so the teacher will have to send me home.

I was trying to read your mind so I can pass tomorrow's test.

That's my trouble—I wasn't.

Do you mean me personally or the character in my head with a red suit and pitchfork?

You don't know? Aren't you supposed to be psychic?

You mean now, or when you started yelling at me?

My mind works in mysterious ways—so sometimes even I'm baffled by it.

I can't recall what I was thinking, but now I'm thinking it would be nice to be invisible.

Why do you keep changing the TV channels?

Because left alone, they'll never change.

I accidentally glued my finger to the remote.

Are you feeling all right? The TV isn't even on.

I guess I'm just flipping out.

I haven't the remotest idea what you're talking about.

I'm not changing them. Our TV satellite must have fallen out of its geosynchronous orbit.

Ask Casper. He has the remote.

I'm exercising for the World's Strongest Thumb competition.

Why are you so dishonest?

I can't help it. I majored in alibi-ology.

A fib never passes my lips. That's why I talk nasally.

I have to write *something* in my diary.

It's the only way I can pass Detention 101.

I never fib—no, that's not true.

I'm not gonna take that question lying down.

I promised never to tell. Well, all right, see it's like this . . . .

Why are you failing all your classes?

When opportunity knocked at my door—I wasn't home.

Because I keep getting caught when I cheat.

I started at the bottom—and stayed there.

Because I never make the same mistake twice. I keep making new ones every day.

I'm the role model for the class dunce.

Somebody has to keep up the family tradition.

I'm not failing all my classes. I got an A in study hall.

The answer to that question fails me.

Did I do something wrong, Officer?

No, today we're giving out tickets for doing things right.

No, I'm giving a ticket to this crazy street because it's going the wrong way.

Yes, I'm with the fashion police and I don't think those white socks go with your orange sandals.

No, you're the five-hundredth person this year to break the speed limit and I want to give you this check for a million dollars.

No, I just got tired of lugging around this fat ticket book, so I decided to make it a little thinner.

Is this really a fire drill?

No, that's the school band practicing for the big game.

No, the school choir has a new soprano.

No, this is an asteroid-might-hit-the-Earth-any day-now drill.

No, I think that's the principal's car alarm going off again.

No, it's a new hearing test, and they're giving it to all the students at once.

No, the janitor installed a new doorbell, but I think he went a little overboard.

Are you a gossip?

Yes, I like letting the chat out of the bag.

Yes, I like to be first with the worst.

Yes, I burn my scandals at both ends.

Yes, I'm developing a keen sense of rumor.

Yes, why tell a lie when the truth will do more damage.

Yes, I just can't leave bad enough alone.

No, and tell everyone you heard it from me first.

Of course not. By the way, is it true you were kept after school yesterday?

Are you vacuuming?

No, it's a new arm-exercise device for bigger biceps.

I was, but now I'm just trying to coax the cat out of the bag.

No, the carpet was bad so I'm beating it.

No I'm just rearranging the dust.

No, it's rabbit season and I'm hunting dust bunnies.

No, I just have it on to drown out my sister's singing.

No, it's an indoor metal detector. I'll give you a third of everything I find.

No, it's an alien life form I'm trying to bring under control.

Yes, and then I'm going to give myself a good cleaning, too.

Is that a Ouija board?

Hold on while I get the answer.

Yes, and your departed uncle says he knows you broke that window.

No, it's a skateboard with numbers and letters.

No, it's a telephone directory from the spirit world.

No, it's a new flat screen TV.

No, it's not an Ouija board; it's a smorgasbord for termites.

No, it's an answering machine for ghosts.

Not Ouija. It's a squeegee board. It predicts how often you should clean your windows.

Yes, it is a Ouija board. We tried predicting the future with a diving board but ended up all wet.

Does anyone besides me know what a ringing phone means?

It means you don't have an answering machine.

Maybe it means they've lost your beeper number.

It means your attempts to stop telemarketers have failed again.

So many questions—let's check the answering machine.

Sorry, I must have been absent for that lecture. Do tell—what *does* a ringing phone mean?

Yes, it means other people are trying to annoy us.

Was that the phone? I thought the hamster's hearing aid needed batteries again.

Yes, it means the principal is calling to find out why I skipped out on detention.

It means somebody called the wrong number.

7. Cooked-up Comebacks

Do you think I made the chili too hot?

Can you repeat that? My ears just melted!

Compared to a five-alarm fire, no.

Not a bit, but please hand me another spoon; this one melted.

No, I always lift my tongue with a pot holder.

No, and to think scientists say they have no idea what it's like to stand on the surface of the sun.

No, steam always escapes from my nose.

We'll let the fire department decide.

Must you chew with your mouth open?

Yes, my tongue is afraid of the dark.

Yes, you always say you like to keep an eye on what I'm eating.

Yes, Dad taught me well, didn't he?

Yes, I'm conducting a science experiment on salivation.

Yes, isn't it amazing all the different colors that foods can form?

Are you eating with your elbows on the table?

Well, aren't we having elbow macaroni tonight?

No, those are my stunt double's elbows.

Yes, but I washed them.

It's the only way I can keep the dog from licking them.

Is that a waffle?

No, it's a pancake with an attitude.

Waffle? This is my second-semester project in sculpture class.

No, it's a square boomerang.

No, it's the first wheel invented by a Stone Age dolt.

Yes, and I personally made each dent with my fingers. Wanna bite?

Did you pack your lunch today?

No, I just carry around this paper bag for show.

I don't know—the science teacher dissected it before I could take a bite.

Yes, do you want to switch? I'll take your lunch and you can eat mine and go home sick.

Are you loading the dishwasher?

No, I'm washing my Frisbee collection.

Yes, I'm the official discus washer for the Olympics.

No, I'm just trying to drown some leftover macaroni.

No, it's a time machine. I'm sending these eating utensils back to the cavemen.

Yes, we wash them once a year, whether they need it or not.

Yes, my mom didn't like it when I had the dogs just lick the plates clean.

Table for how many?

One hundred twelve. We like to change seats every few minutes.

One. My dog will sit on my shoulders.

I don't know; I can't count that high.

Two. One for me and one for my monkey.

Actually, that'll be seven tables—one for each course.

Sixteen. That's about right for a game of Monopoly, isn't it?

It's hard to say. You never know who's going to turn up at these séances.

Table for two, but we'd like four chairs so we can prop up our feet.

Skip the table. We're as hungry as horses—we'll just eat standing up.

Where are you putting all that food?

My leg is hollow.

It's not me. My imaginary playmate keeps picking off my plate.

I'm part hamster. Here—check my cheeks.

I'm slipping most of the meat to my pet crocodile under the table.

Are you making s'mores?

Yes, you could say we're s'moring.

No, were making mudslide dioramas from chocolate.

Yes, don't you think it's a hot idea?

No, were making bait for Bigfoot.

S'more or less.

No, I'm conducting an experiment on how fast plastic can melt inside a graham cracker.

No, we're torturing marshmallows.

Are you going to eat that?

No, I was trying to see if I could watch it get cold!

No, I'm just having a staring contest with the black-eyed peas.

No, I was seeing how long you'd go without saying anything about it!

No, I'm going to have it bronzed and put on my mantle.

I never eat my science experiments.

No, I'm going to put it inside a pyramid, then check to see if it's still fresh in a hundred years.

No, I'm going to plant it in my garden and see what sprouts.

Yes, but only if it makes me sick and I can get out of finals tomorrow.

No, I'm going to stare at it until it gets impatient and bites me on the nose.

Yes, but first I'm going to need a chisel.

No, I'm going to toss it to the dog. If he brings it back, then I'll eat it.

No, I'm going to teach it to do some tricks. "Sit, Stay! Good boy!"

No, I don't like to eat things older than I am.

Is the cafeteria food any good?

Yes, it's good enough to be listed at the poison control.

No, it's terrible and guaranteed to send you to the nurse's office.

No, but the Styrofoam trays are outstanding.

Yes, that's why an ambulance is always standing by.

Yes, but be sure and keep a fly swatter handy.

Yes, I'm saving up enough of it to make my own toxic waste dump.

Yes, the meatballs are especially good for batting practice.

Why do you serve vegetables every day?

There are no vegetables on that tray. The green stuff is old meat loaf and the gray stuff is prune pudding.

Because the pizza delivery guy is afraid to come here.

Because we're slaves to the food pyramid.

Because radical vegetarian terrorists have gained control of the kitchen.

I serve vegetables because I can't find tennis balls.

I'm setting a trap for the celery stalker.

I promised Moo-Moo the Cow safe passage to a vegetarian resort.

8. Health Ha-ha's

Is that a permanent tattoo?

Yes, the tattoo is permanent, but I'm not.

No, it comes right off with sandpaper and a good wire brush.

Not really, since I haven't finished paying for it yet.

No, it's a clip-on tattoo.

No, it's a state-of-the-art high-fashion hologram!

No, it's an iron-on.

Yes, but only the outline. I colored the rest with crayons.

Did you get a haircut?

No, it's autumn and I'm shedding.

No, I got my head stuck in the blender.

Yes, it's the latest buzz!

No, did you get new contact lenses?

Now do you know why we should never play with matches?

Yes, it's supposed to ward off vampires.

Yes, the school has chosen me to be the official mascot—the bald eagle.

No, I always lose my hair when I get a bad report card.

Why did you dye your hair white?

It was an accident; my dad put too much chlorine in the pool.

I was tired of it being purple.

People kept telling me to lighten up.

I got my head stuck in a jar of marshmallow cream.

I didn't dye it; I watched too many scary movies.

Isn't it cool! It's my new Abominable Snowman cut.

Have you grown since I last saw you?

Seeing as it was at breakfast, I don't think so.

No, you've shrunk since I last saw you.

Yes, but only my toenails.

Yes, and it's big of you to say so.

Yes, last summer I grew tomatoes and corn and asparagus.

Yes, the world is expanding and I along with it.

No, I accidentally put on my little brother's clothes.

Yes, everyone says I'm getting too big for my britches.

No, I think there's a disturbance in our gravity.

No, the sky is falling.

Yes, it must have been those magic beans I swallowed.

No, my dad did all our laundry in very hot water.

Why don't you ask my elevator shoes?

Yes and some day I hope to really measure up.

No, I'm wearing stilts. Didn't you hear I joined the circus?

Yes, it's about time you had someone to look up to.

Why do you have a bandage on your finger?

After I cut my foot, I thought a bandage on my finger would help.

Because I couldn't find one big enough to go around my head.

It's the only way I can keep my ring from falling off.

I'd rather not talk about it. It's a rather sticky situation.

That's not a bandage. It's my pet flatworm.

Shh! It's the world's smallest cheat sheet.

Because the lion wouldn't let go when I screamed.

It's there to remind me not to answer idiotic questions.

Was that your stomach rumbling?

Yes, and any second an alien is going to burst out.

No, the kids next door in science lab are building a volcano.

No, our house is near a jet runway.

No, it's a chem lab experiment run amok.

Yes, a tribe of tapeworms is partying in my intestines.

Yes, I should really have a plumber check that out.

Are you really that small?

Yes, you haven't seen my brothers Doc, Sneezy, Grumpy, Bashful, Sleepy, and Happy, have you?

I'm not sure. Slip me on a slide and get out the microscope.

I'll let you know when I get done building my hobbit house.

Let me put it this way—last week the cat mistook me for a mouse.

Are you kidding? Last year for Halloween I stuck an eraser on my head and went as pencil.

You'll have to shout. I can't hear you all the way down here.

I don't know. But it sure is irritating when I get stuck to the bottom of a shoe.

Yes, I keep telling my mom I need more after-school snacks.

Are you talking in your sleep?

No, I'm talking in someone else's sleep. That way I don't disturb myself.

No, I'm snoring in Morse code.

No, I'm singing in my sleep. Can't you tell the difference?

No, you're just dreaming I'm talking in my sleep.

Yes, I can speak seven languages, but only when I'm sleeping.

No, that's the dog reading me a bedtime story.

How do I know? I'm fast asleep.

Is the nurse taking your temperature?

Mmmm. Hmm. Um. Hm.

No, the nurse is using this stick to tickle my tongue.

No, it is my new invention. I call it calculator-on-a-stick.

Here's a hint. You're getting warmer.

No, I'm practicing to be a snake charmer. By the way, have you seen a stray cobra?

No, she already took it and now I'm working on getting her to give it back.

No, this is a mini scale. My tongue looked a little fat so the nurse is weighing it.

No, this is my secret pea shooter. Watch out!

No, I'm on a new diet. Instead of celery sticks, I eat glass sticks.

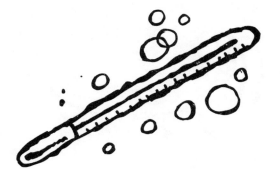

Where are your brains today?

Does it really matter?

Gee, my mind is a blank.

Don't get a head of yourself.

I left them in my locker.

I'm not sure; all I remember is a dark laboratory and someone named Igor.

The biology teacher expelled them.

I lent half of them to my Siamese twin.

Remember when I sneezed really hard an hour ago . . . ?

Do you have braces on your teeth?

No, it's a tracking device so the FBI knows where I am at all times.

It's an antenna for my wristwatch television.

It's a listening device so aliens can spy on us.

No, I'm collecting soda can tabs and keep them in my mouth so they won't get lost.

It's a metallic bar code. I'm $2.95, on sale this week only.

It's an encoding device so that my body can always be identified.

I don't know. I accidentally fell asleep with a magnet under my pillow and I awoke this morning with a metal mouth!

I resent that biting comment.

No, that hubcap I ate for lunch stuck to my gums.

Oh, so that's where I left my watchband.

No, it's an electronic shield to keep the dentist away.

Yes, vampires-in-training wear them before they cut their teeth.

What did you do to your hair?

Birds need nests, don't they?

I thought if I put a lot of mousse in it, I could sprout antlers.

I wanted to be sure it was greasy enough to fry chicken in.

Don't ever put your finger in an electrical socket.

I figured, why go to the barber when I can butcher it myself.

Instead of hair mousse, I accidentally slathered on chocolate mousse

Nothing. On the way to school I was struck by a small bolt of lightning.

My hair is the same; I just grew a bigger head.

Nothing. I just rearranged my dandruff.

9. Laffed-Overs

Are you going to the library with all those books?

Yes, these are all the late ones I checked out on your library card.

No, I'm taking them to the ballpark. They help me see over the fence.

No, I'm taking them out for some air.

Yes, and tomorrow I'm taking them to the movies.

No, I'm going past the bully dugout and I figured I could use these as a shield.

Why must you always sit near the window?

I'm into the weather—like whether I'm going to cut class tomorrow.

I'm expecting a message by owl.

My dad's on board the international space station and likes when I wave to him.

I have a solar-powered brain and must sit in direct sunlight.

It is a "pane" to sit anywhere else.

I want to be as far away from the cafeteria as possible.

Is that an ink stain in your pocket?

Yes, my pet octopus isn't potty-trained.

No, I finished last at the paintball tournament at school.

Let's just say my pen has a runny nose.

No, it's a new line of abstract art clothing—you like it?

No, the sheep they made this shirt from had a tattoo.

No, that's the real color of my shirt. The rest of it is the stain.

Oh! I was wondering where I left that slice of blueberry pie.

Is this really you in the photograph?

What, you didn't recognize me without the paper bag on my head?

Hmm, no. I'd say that's a grade school gargoyle.

No, it's a dart board. Want to play a few games?

Duh, you're holding up a mirror.

Yes, I'm developing into a well-rounded person.

No, that's my dog dressed up as me.

No, that's my stunt double.

Why don't you ever teach your dog any tricks?

He doesn't nag me to do my homework, and I
   don't bother him with tricks.

He's saving his energy for college.

Tricks! He's doing one right now. He's
   impersonating me asleep.

Shh! He doesn't know he's a dog.

He knows every trick in the book but now that
   he's older, he forgot where he put the book.

Tricks! He's a malamute, not a magician.

He came with papers that explicitly forbid stupid
   pet tricks.

Is it true you got terrible reviews in the school play?

No, I gave a very moving performance. Everyone moved to the exit.

No, the audience was very polite. In fact, they even covered their mouths when they yawned.

No, I gave the same performance five nights running—I wouldn't dare give it standing still.

That's not true. Only two people hissed—my parents.

No, the audience called for me after the performance. And they would have gotten me—if it hadn't been for the Witness Protection Program.

No, I put my heart and soul into that performance. Too bad I didn't put any acting into it.

That's not true. I drew a line three blocks long— until someone took my chalk away.

Yes, and they were the best reviews I ever got.

Yes, that's the bad news. The good news is I got plenty of tomatoes.

Yes, I played a very convincing dead body—until I moved.

Yes, and I was just a stagehand, too.

Yes, that's what I get for acting alongside you!

Why are you so full of yourself?

I accidentally fell asleep under a spigot.

Blame it on that sponge I swallowed at the beach.

I was raised by a pride of lions.

As a baby my only crib mobile was a mirror.

Imitation is the sincerest form of flattery, isn't it?

Somebody ate all the bologna.

I'm not full of myself—I'm half empty.

I'm not always full of myself. Occasionally, I spring a leak.

Are you showing off?

Yes, I have a fun-track mind.

That's why they call me the laugh of the party.

Yes, and my nickname's the Surgeon because I'm a big cut up.

No, I always parachute into the classroom so I won't be late.

No, this gorilla really is my big brother.

I'll give you *all* the details when we get to detention hall.

Why do you keep poking me?

I'm trained to be a household pest.

Sorry, I just had a dream I was on a cattle drive.

You did tell me to get on the stick.

I just had a new finger installed and wanted to see if it works properly.

I'm practicing for the school talent shows—I'm doing the hokey pokey.

It wasn't me. I think your seat is haunted.

I guess I've watched too many of those Pokemon shows.

Are you sitting there?

I can't remember. You see—I have short-term memory . . . . What did you ask?

And there—and there—and there!

Yes, but I'll move. I love standing on my head.

No, I'm saving this seat for a three-hundred-pound Sumo wrestler.

No, but my other personality will be along in a moment and he likes this seat.

Yes, and here's a picture I took of me just in case you're wondering who's sitting here.

No, my imaginary friend is.

Is that a bored look in my classroom?

No, your teaching is so compelling, you've put me in a trance.

Yes, I'm trying to match the thirty other faces in this room.

No, I always yawn when I'm paying attention.

No, this is what I look like when I wake up from my nap.

No, I'm blurred. I think I lost one of my contacts.

No, but give me a few erasers and I'll get rid of that board look.

No, that's my "Life of the Party Look."

No, that's my impression of me in Madame Toussard's Wax Museum.

Bored, no. Hypnotized, yes.

After that great performance do you have a swelled head?

Yes, and I would appreciate it if you treated me like any other great person.

I wouldn't call it a swelled head—let's just say it's a halo.

Yes, every time I look in the mirror I take a bow.

Yes, I could make a fortune renting it out as a balloon.

Let me put it this way. On my last birthday I sent my parents an e-mail of congratulations.

Yes, all my paintings are self-portraits.

Yes, I'm so conceited, I have my X rays retouched.

Yes, everyone worships me and so do I.

Am I supposed to pick a card?

Yes, and then you're supposed to look at it and try to guess what it is. Do you think you can do that?

No, you're supposed to take all of them, and then I'll guess every card you took.

No, I'm just trying to hide behind them so no one will notice me.

No, you're supposed to help me get this glue off my fingers!

No, you're supposed to say, "What a lovely impression of a peacock tail!"

Is that your final answer?

I'm not sure. Is that your final question?

No, my final answer can be found on the guy who copied my paper.

Would you take a definite maybe?

Um, what's the name of the class again?

Until I think of another one, yes.

Could you be more specific?

What are your feelings on second chances?

No, but this is the last quip of the book.

Index